Exploration & Encounters

# The Spanish Conquests in the New World

Peter Chrisp

Thomson Learning
New York

# Exploration & Encounters
## The Search for the East
## Voyages to the New World
## The Spanish Conquests in the New World
## The Search for a Northern Route

Cover pictures: Ptolemy's world map, recreated in 1486, and an Aztec featherwork shield showing a waterbeast with a sacrificial knife in its jaws.
Title page picture: Montezuma, ruler of the Aztecs, sees a blazing comet in the sky. From the Aztec history, in which the comet is a sign that the Aztec Empire will soon be destroyed.

First published in the United States in 1993 by
Thomson Learning
115 Fifth Avenue
New York, NY 10003

First published in 1993 by Wayland (Publishers) Ltd.

Library of Congress Cataloging-in-Publication Data
Chrisp, Peter.
  The Spanish conquests in the New World / Peter Chrisp.
     p.   cm. (Exploration & encounters, 1450-1550)
  Includes bibliographical references and indexes.
  Summary : A history of Spanish exploration and conquests in America, with an emphasis on Cortés and Pizarro.
  ISBN 1-56847-123-8 : $14.95
  1. Latin America – History – To 1600 – Juvenile literature. 2. America – Discovery and exploration – Spanish – Juvenile literature.
3. Conquerors – America – History – 16th century – Juvenile literature.
4. Conquerors – Spain – History – 16th century – Juvenile literature.
5. Indians – History – 16th century – Juvenile literature. [1. Latin America – History. 2. America – Discovery and exploration – Spanish.
3. Explorers.] I. Title. II. Series.
F1411.C57   1993                          93-24396

Printed in Italy

## Picture acknowledgments
The publishers would like to thank the following for allowing their pictures to be reproduced in this book: Biblioteca Medicea Laurenziana, Florence 12, 14, 18, 19, 26, 27, 28, 29; Biblioteca Nacional, Madrid 6; Bibliothèque Nationale, Paris 7; The Board of Trustees of the Royal Armouries, London 15; Bodleian Library, Oxford *title page*, 8, 11, 17, 20, 24, 25, 39; Bridgeman Art Library 9, 13, 21; Glasgow University Library 42, 43, 44; Michael Holford *cover* (map); Marion and Tony Morrison 16, 33, 34, 35, 36, 38, 40, 41, 45; Wayland Picture Library 4; Werner Forman Archive *cover* (main), 22, 23, 31.

## SOURCES OF QUOTES
Page 9: Francisco Lopez de Gomara, *Cortés. The Life of the Conqueror by his Secretary* translated by L. B. Simpson (University of California Press, 1965), p. 24-25.
Page 15: Extract from the *Codex Florentino* in Miguel Leon-Portilla (ed.), *The Broken Spears. The Aztec Account of the Conquest of Mexico* (Beacon Press, 1992), p. 30-31.
Page 17: Bernal Diaz, *The Conquest of New Spain* translated by J. M. Cohen (Penguin, 1963), p. 140.
Page 19: *Codex Florentino* in Leon-Portilla, op. cit., p. 35-36.
Page 21: Bernal Diaz, op. cit., p. 216.
Page 23: *Codex Florentino* in Leon-Portilla, op. cit., p. 66-68.
Page 25: *The Chronicle of Fray Francisco de Aguilar* in *The Conquistadors. First Person Accounts of the Conquest of Mexico* translated by Patricia de Fuentes (Cassell, 1964), p. 155.
Page 26: *Codex Florentino* in Leon-Portilla, op. cit., p. 92-93.
Page 29: Poem from the *Annals of Tlatelolco* in Leon-Portilla, op. cit., p. 137.
Page 31: Francisco de Montejo, quoted by Robert S. Chamberlain, *The Conquest and Colonization of Yucatan, 1517–1550* (Octagon Books, 1966), p. 165.
Page 35: Garcilaso de la Vega, *Royal Commentaries of the Incas* translated by Harold Livermore (University of Texas Press, 1966), Part One, p. 329-31.
Page 37: Felipé Waman Puma, quoted by Ronald Wright, *Stolen Continents. The Indian Story* (John Murray, 1992), p. 75.
Page 42: Bishop Diego de Landa, quoted by Wright, op. cit., p. 168.
Page 45: Cieza de Leon, quoted by Wright, op. cit., p. 13.

# CONTENTS

**Note on pictures:**
Many pictures here are by native people from the time of the Spanish Conquest. Some were kept as records and others were sent back to Spain.

# Spaniards in the New World

In 1492, Spanish ships first crossed the Atlantic Ocean and reached the islands of the Caribbean. Their captain, Christopher Columbus, was looking for the Indies, the old European name for the

Christopher Columbus, who was sure that the Caribbean islands were part of Asia

countries in the East. He was sure that the Indies were lands of vast wealth, with cities roofed with gold. By finding a sea route to the Indies, Columbus hoped to make Spain rich and to win fame for himself.

When Columbus reached the Caribbean islands, he was certain that he had found the Indies. He called the Taino people whom he met there "Indians." He sailed along the coast of Cuba, believing it to be China, and then arrived at a lush green island that he called "Hispaniola," the Spanish island. To Columbus, this seemed a perfect place to start a Spanish settlement.

A year later, Columbus sailed back to Hispaniola with 1,200 Spanish settlers, all hoping to make themselves rich with the gold of the Indies.

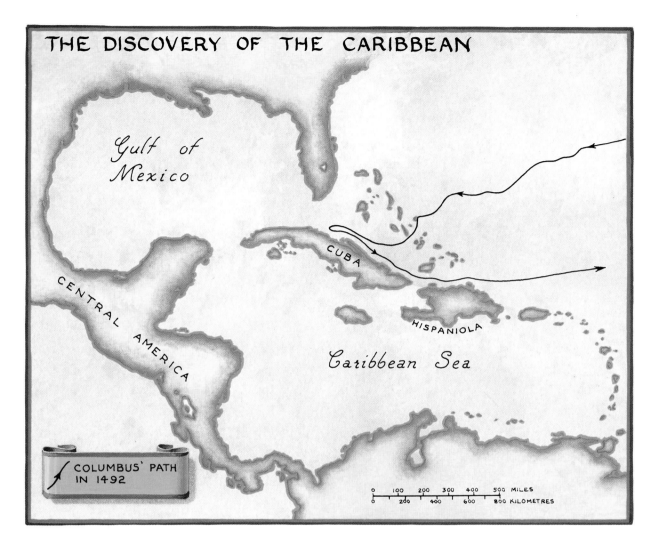

## THE DISCOVERY OF THE CARIBBEAN

Gulf of Mexico

CENTRAL AMERICA

CUBA

HISPANIOLA

Caribbean Sea

COLUMBUS' PATH IN 1492

| 0 | 100 | 200 | 300 | 400 | 500 MILES |
| 0 | 200 | 400 | 600 | 800 KILOMETRES |

They were quickly disappointed, for there was hardly any gold on Hispaniola.

While the settlers were looking for gold, Spanish explorers were sailing the Caribbean, still looking for the rich cities of Asia. They found a large area of mainland to the south and west of the Caribbean islands, but it did not match any descriptions of China. The Spaniards realized they had found a "new world" – a land of which no one in Europe had ever heard. This "new world" came to be called America.

# War Against the Tainos

From their earliest days on Hispaniola, the Spaniards expected the Tainos to work for them, to bring them food and to mine for gold. They saw this as their reward for finding land for the Spanish king and for bringing Christianity to the Tainos. They believed that their own way of life was better than that of the Tainos, and that this gave them the right to order the Tainos around. The Tainos grew tired of working for the Spaniards and tried to fight them, but they had no chance against European weapons. Many were killed. Even more died of diseases brought to the island by the Spanish and from overworking.

Meanwhile, more settlers came from Spain, hoping for a better life. By 1510, so many Tainos had died or fled from Hispaniola that there were not enough left to work for all the Spaniards. Since they had still not found much gold, many settlers decided to move on to another part of the "new world."

Diego Velazquez, conqueror of Cuba and first governor of the island

6

In 1511, Diego Velazquez and 300 men sailed to the neighboring island, Cuba. The Cuban Tainos knew what to expect from the Spanish – many Tainos had fled there from Hispaniola, with news of what was happening on the island. The Cubans fought back from the start. But, like the Hispaniolan Tainos, they had no chance against the Spaniards' guns and swords.

Spanish soldiers on the march, using local people to carry their supplies. This Mexican picture shows how the Spaniards appeared to the people of the "new world."

The Spanish invaders quickly conquered Cuba and divided the land among themselves. They built towns on the island and began to farm and to mine for gold. As on Hispaniola, all the hard work was done by the Tainos.

# Expeditions to the Mainland

From Cuba, Spanish ships set out to search for gold in new lands. In 1517, Francisco de Cordoba sailed to Yucatan on the mainland, where he found beautifully made stone buildings. Cordoba was pleased to see that the local people, the Maya, wore fine cotton clothes and had gold ornaments. The mainland people were clearly richer than the Tainos. Unfortunately, the Maya were not pleased to see Cordoba. They attacked him and forced him to flee.

He struggled back to Cuba and died of his wounds.

In 1518, Juan de Grijalva led a second expedition to the mainland (modern Mexico). He traded with the local people for gold ornaments.

When Grijalva returned to Cuba, the Spaniards there were very excited to see the gold. Eleven ships, carrying about 550 well-armed men and sixteen horses, were quickly prepared. The leader of this expedition was a man named Hernan Cortés.

The mainland people were astonished when they first saw Spanish ships. They described them as floating towers or mountains.

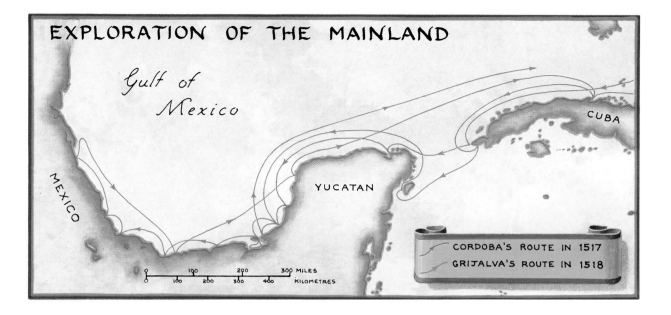

## EXPLORATION OF THE MAINLAND

Gulf of Mexico

MEXICO

YUCATAN

CUBA

0  100  200  300 MILES
0  100  200  300  400 KILOMETRES

CORDOBA'S ROUTE IN 1517
GRIJALVA'S ROUTE IN 1518

Before setting off, Cortés made a speech to his men. According to his secretary, Gomara, this is what Cortés said:

*I am setting out on a great and beautiful enterprise, which will be famous in times to come. I know in my heart that we shall take vast and wealthy lands and people, such as have never been seen before.... We are going to fight a just and good war, which will bring us fame. Almighty God, in whose name and faith it will be waged, will give us victory.*

*If you do not abandon me, as I shall not abandon you, I shall make you, in a short time, the richest of all men who have crossed the seas.*

Hernan Cortés hoped to get rich and win fame by conquering the mainland.

9

# The Aztec Empire

Cortés did not know it, but he was sailing toward the coast of a great empire, ruled by a people called the Aztecs. About ten million people lived in the Aztec Empire. They had been conquered by the Aztecs in a series of wars.

The Aztecs did not rule these people directly. The conquered towns were allowed to run their own affairs as long as they gave regular payments of "tribute" to the Aztecs – food, precious stones, gold, and brightly colored feathers. They hated having to pay the tribute, but the Aztecs were too strong to be disobeyed.

The Aztecs' home was a great city called Tenochtitlan. It was built on marshy islands

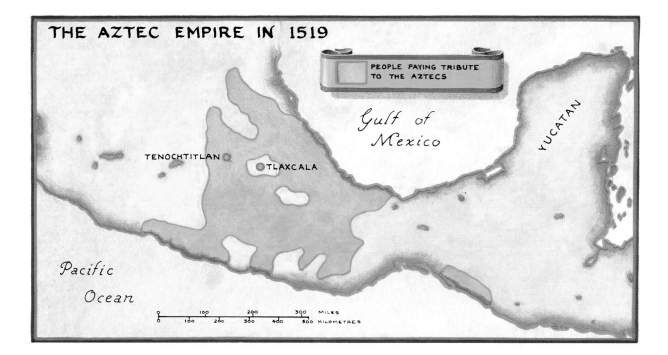

THE AZTEC EMPIRE IN 1519

PEOPLE PAYING TRIBUTE TO THE AZTECS

Gulf of Mexico

YUCATAN

TENOCHTITLAN

TLAXCALA

Pacific Ocean

MILES
0    100    200    300
0  100  200  300  400  500 KILOMETRES

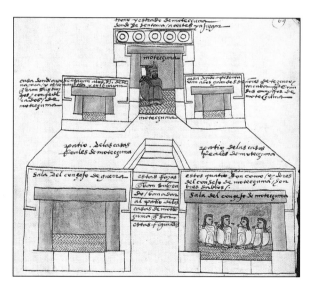

*Above* Aztec picture books show many scenes of ordinary life. Here naughty children are held over smoking chilis.

*Below* Montezuma, the Aztec ruler, sits in his palace. The men at the bottom are his advisers.

in the middle of a lake called Texcoco, and was joined to the mainland by three stone causeways. Fresh water was brought to the city from the lakeside in stone channels called aqueducts. The center of the city was full of palaces and temples. More than 300,000 people lived in Tenochtitlan, making it one of the biggest cities in the world at that time.

In 1519, the ruler of the Aztec Empire was a man named Montezuma, which means "Angry Lord." He was a feared and respected war leader who had ruled the Aztecs for seventeen years. Montezuma was also very religious. He was like a high priest, whose job it was to oversee the ceremonies of the Aztec religion.

# Aztec Religion

The Aztecs believed that there were many different gods, who watched over different parts of life. The most important were Huitzilopochtli, the god of war, and Tlaloc, the god of rain. Huitzilopochtli was the special protector of the Aztec people.

They believed he helped them conquer a great empire. Tlaloc provided the rain that made the crops grow. Without the help of Tlaloc, the Aztecs believed they would starve. These two gods shared a great temple in the center of Tenochtitlan.

Huitzilopochtli, the god of war (left) and Tlaloc, the god of rain, storms, and lightning

The Aztecs thought that gods, like people, needed to be fed in order to stay strong and healthy. If they were not fed, the gods would lose their power. Then the world would come to an end.

The Aztec way of feeding the gods was by giving them the blood of prisoners captured in battle. They led the prisoners up the steps of the great temple and then sacrificed them by cutting out and eating their hearts. The Aztecs said that it was an honor for a brave prisoner to feed the gods in this way.

In battle, the Aztecs did not fight to kill their enemies. They preferred to take them prisoner so that they could sacrifice them later. This custom caused big problems for the Aztecs when they came to fight the Spaniards. The Spaniards did not take prisoners in battle, but simply killed their enemies.

An Aztec painting of human sacrifice. While warriors dance around the temple, the body of their sacrificed prisoner lies on the steps, chopped into pieces.

# The Spaniards Land

The Aztec messengers offered beautiful gifts to Cortés.

In April 1519, Cortés's ships landed on the Mexican coast. News of their arrival quickly reached the Aztecs.

Montezuma sent messengers to greet the strangers with rich gifts and to find out who, or what, they were. Were they men or gods?

One of Cortés's men had once been shipwrecked among the Maya and could speak Mayan. Cortés also knew a woman from Mexico named Malinalli who could speak both Mayan and the Aztec language. Through these two, Cortés spoke to the Aztecs.

Cortés told the messengers that he wished to visit Montezuma and be his friend. To impress them, he ordered the Spanish cavalry to gallop up and down the beach, and a cannon was fired. The Aztecs fell to the ground, terrified by the smoke and the noise.

Once they got over the shock, the messengers raced back to report to Montezuma.

The Aztecs remembered their past through picture books and stories, which people learned by heart and passed on. Later, Spanish friars wrote down the Aztec stories in books. One such book, the *Codex Florentino*, includes the coming of Cortés.

This extract is from the messengers' report about the Spaniards and their horses:

*They dress in metal and wear metal hats on their heads. Their deer carry them on their backs wherever they wish to go. These deer are as tall as the roof of a house.*

*The strangers' bodies are completely covered, so that only their faces can be seen. Their skin is white. They have yellow hair, though some have black. Their beards are long and yellow, and their moustaches are also yellow. Their hair is curly with fine strands.*

The armor worn by the Spaniards must have made them look like creatures from another world.

# The Journey Inland

The people who lived on the coast welcomed the Spaniards and told them about the great power and wealth of the Aztecs. They said that many of the peoples of Mexico hated the Aztecs and would welcome the chance to overthrow them.

Cortés decided to head for the Aztec capital. In August 1519, the Spaniards started their long journey inland. They traveled on foot through snow-covered mountains and across deserts to a land called Tlaxcala.

The Tlaxcalans had never been conquered by the Aztecs. They had often fought against them but always managed to keep their freedom. Cortés was hoping to win the Tlaxcalans to his side.

The Tlaxcalans refused Cortés's offer of friendship and attacked the Spaniards.

When the Spaniards rode past Mt. Popocatapetl, the volcano was belching smoke. The Spanish were amazed, for they had never seen a live volcano. Cortés sent ten men up the mountain to find out where the smoke came from, but they were forced back by whirling ash.

One of Cortés's soldiers, Bernal Diaz, described the fight with the Tlaxcalans:

*We were four hundred, of whom many were sick and wounded, and we stood in the middle of a plain swarming with Indian warriors. Moreover we knew that they had come determined to leave none of us alive except those who were to be sacrificed to their idols. The Indians charged us in such numbers that only by a miracle of swordplay were we able to drive them back. One thing alone saved our lives. They were so massed and so many that every shot caused havoc among them.*

For two weeks, the Spaniards had to fight daily battles against Tlaxcalan warriors. However, thanks to their horses, guns, and swords, the Spaniards always managed to win these battles. The Tlaxcalans saw that they could not beat the Spaniards, and so they offered to be their friends.

This Tlaxcalan picture shows the Spaniards making peace with the Tlaxcalans and setting up a cross in their town.

# The Gods Are Coming!

In Tenochtitlan, Montezuma heard reports about the strangers with growing alarm. He was still not sure if they were gods or men. It was bad enough that they were on their way to his city. What was worse was that they had joined forces with his greatest enemies, the Tlaxcalans.

*Left* Cortés is greeted by Aztec messengers on the way to Tenochtitlan.

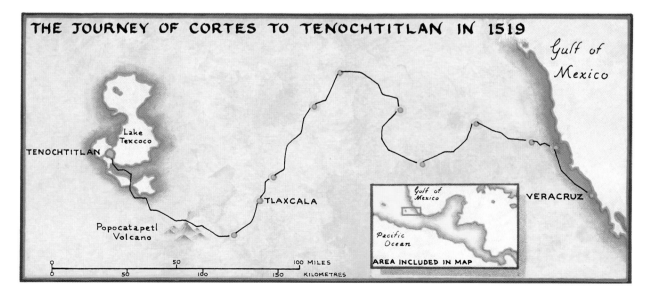

THE JOURNEY OF CORTES TO TENOCHTITLAN IN 1519

Gulf of Mexico

Lake Texcoco

TENOCHTITLAN

TLAXCALA

VERACRUZ

Popocatapetl Volcano

Gulf of Mexico

Pacific Ocean

AREA INCLUDED IN MAP

50          100 MILES

50      100      150   KILOMETRES

While the Spaniards were on their journey, Cortés and Montezuma sent friendly messages to each other. Each man hid his real feelings. Montezuma hid his fear and pretended to be pleased that Cortés was coming. Cortés pretended that all he wanted to do was to visit Montezuma and talk with him. In fact, he hoped to take over the Aztec Empire.

The Aztec history described Montezuma's state of mind:

*Montezuma was filled with terror, not knowing what would happen to the city. The people were also terrified. There were meetings and arguments and gossip in the street. The people went about with their heads bowed down and greeted each other with tears.*

*It was also at this time that the Spaniards asked many questions about Montezuma.*

*They asked the villagers, "Is he a young or an old man?"*

*When Montezuma heard that the "gods" were asking about him and wished to see him face to face, he was filled with fear. He wanted to run away and hide. But he could not do it. He had lost his strength and his spirit. Therefore he did nothing but wait.*

The Aztec artists showed in pictures how Montezuma was in doubt. Here he cannot decide whether to run away or hide in a cave.

# The Spaniards at Tenochtitlan

On November 8, 1519, the Spaniards finally reached Lake Texcoco and saw Tenochtitlan. Now they had to cross the stone causeway, which led across the lake from the south to the Aztec city.

Riding along the causeway, Cortés and his men saw a procession coming toward them. It was Montezuma, carried on a litter, surrounded by his chief lords, who held garlands of flowers. They wrapped the flowers around the Spaniards' necks, and Montezuma made a speech of welcome.

*Left* This is the very first Spanish map of Tenochtitlan. Aztec canoes are paddled on the lake.

*Opposite* This Spanish painting shows Montezuma and his lords coming to greet the Spaniards.

Montezuma then took the Spaniards into the city, to one of the royal palaces. They were to be his honored guests. Meanwhile, the Tlaxcalans camped in the palace courtyard.

 Bernal Diaz was one of Cortés's soldiers. As an old man, he remembered the first view of Tenochtitlan, as the Spaniards rode across the causeway:

*The causeway was so crowded with people that we could hardly get through. They came in canoes from all parts of the lake to look at us. No wonder, since they had never seen horses or men like us before!*

*With such wonderful sights to gaze on we did not know what to say, or if what we saw was real. On the lakeside there were many cities, and on the lake many more, and before us was the great city of Mexico* [Tenochtitlan]. *As for us, we were scarcely 400 strong, and we well remembered the warnings we had been given to beware of entering the city, since they would kill us as soon as they had us inside. What men in all the world have shown such daring?*

# Montezuma Taken Prisoner

The Spaniards spent a week sightseeing in the city, amazed at its wealth. They climbed the steps of the great temple and were horrified by the bloodstained statues of the Aztec gods. The Spaniards were devout Christians and believed that the Aztec religion was devil worship.

The Spaniards were overjoyed when they saw the Aztec ornaments made of gold.

With each day, the Spaniards grew more worried about their safety. Only Montezuma's good will kept the Aztecs from attacking them. How long could this last?

Cortés decided that he would have to capture Montezuma and keep him prisoner. Then he could use him to rule. He took thirty armed Spaniards to Montezuma's palace and arrested the Aztec ruler. Montezuma was shocked to be treated like this. By now, he must have realized that the bearded men were not gods. Even so, he did not resist – the heavily armed Spaniards made it clear that they would kill him if he did not agree to go with them.

The Aztec history tells us how the Spaniards behaved once Montezuma was a prisoner:

*The Spaniards asked Montezuma about the city's wealth. They questioned him closely and demanded gold.*

*Montezuma guided them to it. When they arrived at the treasure house, the riches of gold and feathers were brought out to them: ornaments made of feathers, richly worked shields, gold bracelets and crowns.*

*The Spaniards stripped the feathers from the gold shields. They gathered all the gold into a great mound and set fire to everything else, no matter its value. Then they melted down the gold into bars.*

*Next they went to Montezuma's storehouse, where his personal treasures were kept. The Spaniards grinned like little beasts and patted each other with delight.*

The Aztecs valued beautiful featherwork, like this shield decorated with a water serpent, even more than gold. To the Spaniards, feathers were worthless. Most Aztec featherwork was destroyed.

# The Aztecs Rebel

For six months, Cortés and his men stayed in Tenochtitlan, using Montezuma to give orders to the Aztecs. The Aztecs now hated the Spaniards, but they still obeyed their lord.

In May 1521, the Aztecs held a religious festival, with music and dancing. The Spanish suddenly attacked the dancers, cutting them down with their swords. The killing was ordered by Cortés's second-in-command, Pedro de Alvarado. (Cortés was away, dealing with a rival expedition from Cuba.). He said that the Aztecs had planned an uprising against the Spaniards during the festival.

The heavily armed Spaniards attack the Aztec dancers. They block all the doors so that no one can escape.

Now the Spaniards are trapped. Their palace is surrounded by furious Aztec warriors.

The furious Aztecs attacked the Spaniards inside the palace. Cortés now returned and sent Montezuma onto the roof to calm his people, but they just shouted and threw stones. One stone hit Montezuma, who fell to the ground. Later, he was found dead. The Spaniards said that the stone had killed him. The Aztecs said that he was murdered by the Spaniards.

Cortés was trapped in the palace. He decided to break out of Tenochtitlan, so late one night the Spaniards crept out of the palace. They were spotted at the western causeway and the alarm was raised. Within minutes, Aztec warriors were attacking them from all directions.

One of the Spanish soldiers, Alonso de Aguilar, described the retreat across the causeway: *The Indians followed us with great fury, shooting arrows... and wounding us with their swords. Many Spaniards... fell, some dead and some wounded, and others who fainted from fright. It was heartbreaking to see our companions dying and to see how the Indians carried them off to tear them to pieces.*

# Cortés Gets a New Army

After the Spaniards were driven out of Tenochtitlan, a terrible outbreak of smallpox spread through the city. Smallpox was a disease that had been brought to the "new world" by the Spaniards. Alonso de Aguilar, one of Cortés's soldiers, later wrote:

*When the Christians were exhausted from war, God saw fit to send the Indians smallpox.*

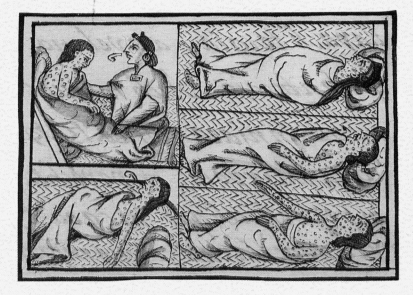

The Aztec history describes the effect of the disease:

*A great plague broke out here in Tenochtitlan. It began to spread, striking everywhere in the city and killing a vast number of our people. Sores broke out on our faces, our breasts, our bellies. We were covered with agonizing sores from head to foot. The illness was so dreadful that no one could walk or move. Many died from this plague, and many others died from hunger. They could not get up to search for food, and everyone else was too sick to care for them.*

The Aztecs began to die from smallpox, an illness they had never seen before.

There were great celebrations, with music and dancing, when the Spaniards were driven from the city.

Cortés and the Spanish survivors made for Tlaxcala, the city of their allies. Luckily for Cortés, the Tlaxcalans stayed friendly to the Spaniards. In Tlaxcala they were able to rest and recover from their wounds.

Cortés now sent messages to Hispaniola and Cuba, asking for fresh men, horses, and weapons. He was determined to return to conquer Tenochtitlan with a new army.

Meanwhile, the Aztecs celebrated the defeat of the Spaniards, thinking they had seen the last of them. Their new ruler died and was replaced by Cuauhtemoc, the young nephew of Montezuma. Cuauhtemoc soon learned that the Spaniards had not gone away. In May 1521, Cortés was on his way back, with his new army.

# The Battle for Tenochtitlan

Cortés spent months preparing for the final attack on Tenochtitlan. He was joined by about 100,000 warriors, who came from Tlaxcala and other towns in Mexico. They were all eager to take part in the downfall of the Aztecs.

First Cortés captured the towns around the lake, to keep them from helping the Aztecs. He built 12 small ships, each armed with a cannon, to fight on the lake. He also destroyed the aqueducts that brought fresh water to the city. His aim was to cut off the Aztecs from all sources of food and water.

At last the attack on the city began. Even though they were weakened by hunger, thirst, and disease, the Aztecs would not surrender. For four months they fought their enemies in the streets of Tenochtitlan. The end finally came in August 1521, when only a tiny corner of the city was left in Aztec hands. Cuauhtemoc was captured and his warriors gave up the fight.

Cortés launched a fleet of small ships on the lake. The Aztec war canoes had no chance against these ships.

28

The Aztecs fought hard but were defeated by the Spaniards.

The defeat was described in an Aztec poem, composed in the 1520s:

*Broken spears lie in the roads;*
*we have torn our hair in our grief.*
*The houses are roofless now, and their walls*
*are red with blood.*
*We have beaten our hands in despair*
*against the mud-brick walls,*
*for our inheritance, our city, is lost and dead.*
*The shields of our warriors were its defense,*
*but they could not save it.*

# The Maya

Following the conquest of the Aztecs, Spanish armies spread out all over Mexico, looking for rich lands to invade. Cortés's fame back in Spain attracted thousands of Spanish soldiers to the "new world." Each one dreamed of gaining wealth as a Spanish conquistador.

In the 1520s, two Spanish armies fought the Maya, the people who lived to the east of the Aztecs. Pedro de Alvarado attacked the Maya who lived in Guatemala. Then Francisco de Montejo invaded Yucatan, where the northern Maya lived.

CAMPAIGNS AGAINST THE MAYA

Gulf of Mexico

MEXICO

YUCATAN

Montejo 1527-8

Montejo 1529-35

Alvarado 1524-30

GUATEMALA

Pacific Ocean

LANDS OF THE MAYA

The Maya were more successful than the Aztecs against the Spaniards. The Maya did not fight in the open, where the Spaniards could use their horses, but hid in forests and set ambushes. They poisoned wells and dug holes to trap the Spaniards' horses.

A pottery figure of a fierce Maya warrior, made six hundred years before the Spaniards arrived in the "new world."

After seven years spent trying to conquer Yucatan, Francisco de Montejo wrote a despairing letter to King Charles of Spain:

*No gold has been found here, nor is there anything else from which advantage can be gained. The inhabitants are the most treacherous in all the lands yet discovered. They never yet killed a Christian except by foul means, nor made war except by trickery. Not once have I questioned them on any matter without them answering "Yes," with the aim of making me leave them and go somewhere else.*

The Maya lived in many separate kingdoms and had no overall ruler, like Montezuma, who could be captured. Therefore they could not be conquered in a single battle. Alvarado took three years to overcome Guatemala. Montejo eventually gave up trying to conquer Yucatan. Only in 1697 was the last Mayan stronghold captured by the Spanish.

# Pizarro

In 1519, the Spaniards built a town called Panama on the Pacific coast of America.

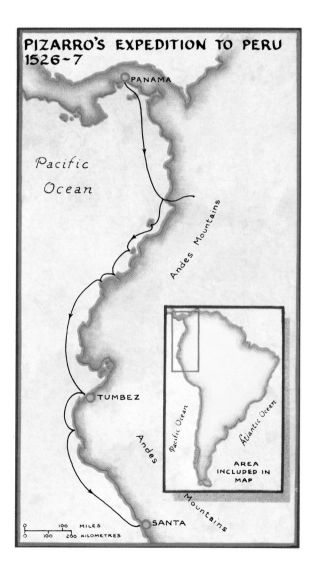

This became a base to explore South America. One of the first settlers at Panama was a tough ex-soldier named Francisco Pizarro. Unlike Cortés, who was well-educated, Pizarro came from a poor background and could not read or write. But, like Cortés, he wanted to win fame and wealth as a conquistador.

In Panama, Pizarro heard rumors of a land of gold to the south, which he thought was called Peru. In 1526, he sailed down the coast with two small ships to try to find it.

One of the ships came across a strange craft – an ocean-going balsa raft carrying beautifully made gold and silver ornaments. Most of the raft's crew jumped overboard, but the Spaniards were able to grab three men, whom they taught to speak Spanish.

32

Sailing farther south, Pizarro came to a well-built city called Tumbez. Here the Spaniards were given a friendly welcome and shown a temple decorated with sheets of gold. Pizarro had found signs of another rich civilization.

Pizarro now made careful preparations to conquer the south. He traveled back to Spain to show the gold ornaments to King Charles and to be made governor of the lands he hoped to conquer. He recruited men and bought horses and weapons. In 1531, he was finally ready. He set out with three ships and 180 men for Peru.

*Above* Francisco Pizarro was sure that a rich civilization could be found in South America.
*Left* The perfectly built stone walls of the Incas. When Pizarro saw walls like these, he knew that he had found what he was looking for.

# The Incas

The people who lived in Peru are called the Incas, after the title of their ruler. He was known as the *Sapa Inca* (sole lord). His empire stretched more than 2,500 miles from north to south.

This huge empire was linked by thousands of miles of well-built roads. These roads were used by Inca armies and the official messengers, who ran in relay carrying orders and news.

The Incas were much better organized than the Aztecs. The *Sapa Inca* controlled the lives of everyone in his lands. Ordinary people had to take turns at fixing the irrigation canals that watered the fields. They built the roads and served in the army. In return, the Inca rulers made sure that no one starved. In times of shortage they gave out food to the people.

The paved roads of the Incas crossed every kind of landscape, from low-lying marshes to steep mountainsides.

The Incas worshiped the sun, the moon, and the earth as gods. The *Sapa Inca* himself was also thought to be a god, a child of the sun.

The Incas had no writing system, but they kept records with lengths of knotted string called *quipus*. Garcilaso de la Vega, son of a conquistador and an Inca princess, described how the *quipus* were used: *The colors showed what subject the thread was about, such as yellow for gold, white for silver and red for warriors...*

They recorded through knots all the tribute brought each year to the **Inca.** They recorded the number of men who went to the wars, how many died in them, and how many were born and died each year. In short, they may be said to have recorded on their knots everything that could be counted.

An Inca drawing showing how a *quipu* was used.

# Atahuallpa

In 1527 the *Sapa Inca*, Huayna Capac, died of smallpox. Two of his sons now fought a war against each other to become the new ruler. This war, which split Peru in two, was a great help to Pizarro. The Incas were too busy fighting each other to take much notice of the small band of Spaniards who had arrived.

The war between the sons ended when one of them, Atahuallpa, captured his

Macchu Picchu, a ruined Inca city high up in the Andes. The Spaniards never found this city. It was abandoned by the Incas and was rediscovered only in 1911.

brother in battle and proclaimed himself the new *Sapa Inca*. The Spaniards heard that Atahuallpa and his army were camped at a town called Cajamarca, high in the Andes mountains. They set off to meet the new ruler.

Atahuallpa was curious to see the foreigners and their strange animals. Unlike Montezuma, he did not think the Spaniards were gods.

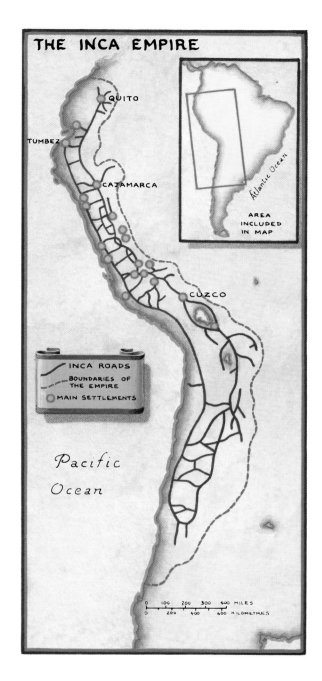

THE INCA EMPIRE

QUITO

TUMBEZ

CAJAMARCA

CUZCO

AREA INCLUDED IN MAP

Atlantic Ocean

INCA ROADS
BOUNDARIES OF THE EMPIRE
MAIN SETTLEMENTS

*Pacific Ocean*

0  100  200  300  400 MILES
0    200    400    600 KILOMETRES

Felipé Waman Puma, a sixteenth-century Inca writer, described the reports that reached Atahuallpa about the strangers: **The strangers did not sleep.** [This was said because they stayed up late at night] **They ate silver and gold, and day and night each one spoke with his papers and writings. And they were all encased [by armor], and their faces completely covered in wool, so that all that could be seen was their eyes.**

He was not afraid of them at all. After all, he had an army of 50,000 warriors with him, while Pizarro had less than 200 men.

# The Capture of the Sapa Inca

In November 1532, the Spaniards rode into the town of Cajamarca, where Atahuallpa had invited them to stay. The *Sapa Inca* was camped outside the town with his great army.

Pizarro knew the story of the capture of Montezuma. He decided to follow Cortés's example and take Atahuallpa prisoner. This was a very bold plan, for the Spaniards were vastly outnumbered by the Inca army.

Atahuallpa sent a message that he would visit the Spaniards with only 5,000 of his men, who would be unarmed. The *Sapa Inca* did not dream that Pizarro was a threat to him.

In the evening, Atahuallpa was carried into the town square on a golden litter, surrounded by his most important nobles. A Spanish

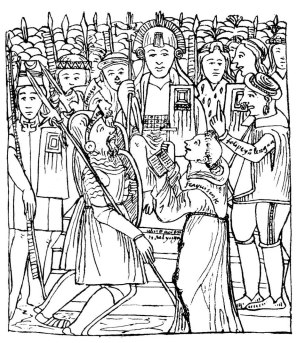

Atahuallpa comes face to face with the Spaniards. He is puzzled by the friar, who hands the Bible to him.

priest went up to the *Sapa Inca* and began to preach to him, waving the Bible. Atahuallpa glanced through the Bible, which meant nothing to him. He threw it impatiently to the ground. At this, the priest spun around and shouted to Pizarro, "At them! At them!"

This was the prearranged signal. A cannon was fired and the Spanish cavalry charged forward waving their swords. Pizarro rode up to the litter and dragged Atahuallpa out by the hair. The *Sapa Inca*'s followers tried to protect him with their bare arms, but they were cut down. The Spaniards slashed so wildly with their swords that Pizarro was wounded in the hand. In minutes it was all over. The *Sapa Inca* was a prisoner of the Spaniards.

A European view of the capture of Atahuallpa.

39

# A Roomful of Gold

Atahuallpa soon realized that what the strangers wanted was gold. He believed that if he gave them enough, he could buy them off. Atahuallpa offered to fill a large room with gold in exchange for his freedom. The Spaniards could not believe their luck and agreed at once.

Atahuallpa was now a prisoner of the Spaniards.

Even though the *Sapa Inca* was a prisoner, he was still obeyed by the people of Peru. He sent orders throughout the land for gold to be brought to Cajamarca. Over the next few months, the temples and palaces of Peru were stripped of their gold ornaments. Eventually about 7 tons of gold and 13 tons of silver were collected. Almost all of it was melted down on the spot.

Atahuallpa had kept his half of the bargain, but Pizarro could not afford to free him. He knew that if he let him go, Atahuallpa might gather his army and attack the Spaniards. The *Sapa Inca* did not realize that the Spaniards could not be bought off. They had come to rule, not just to get gold.

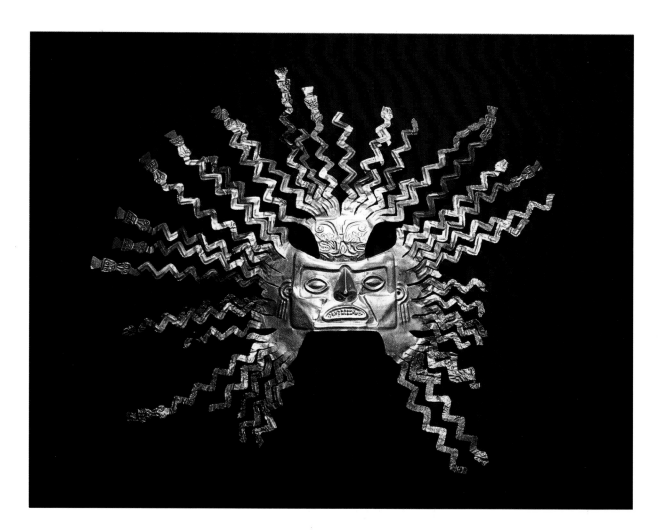

An Inca mask of the sun, made of gold. The Incas called gold the "sweat of the sun." Most Inca gold ornaments were melted down by the Spaniards. Luckily, some pieces survived, mainly in the tombs of rulers.

Pizarro accused Atahuallpa of plotting against him and sentenced him to death. On August 29, 1533, Atahuallpa was strangled.

After Atahuallpa's death, the Spanish took over his empire. However, most of the Spanish conquistadors did not live long enough to enjoy their wealth. They ended up fighting among themselves over who should rule the new lands. Pizarro was murdered by a rival group of Spaniards in 1541.

# The Coming of Christianity

Spanish rule changed life in almost every way for the Indians, as the Spaniards called the local peoples. One great change was that the Indians' old religions were stamped out. All over the conquered lands, temples were destroyed and statues of the gods were smashed. In their place, statues of the Virgin Mary and crosses were set up.

Christian missionaries traveled from Spain to preach their faith. The Indians could

The missionaries were sure that the old religions were devil worship, and they tried to destroy all traces of them. Bishop Diego de Landa of Yucatan described coming across the beautiful painted books of the Maya – the only American people to invent a complete writing system:

*We found a great number of books in these letters of theirs, and because they contained nothing but superstition and lies of the devil, we burned them all, which upset the Indians greatly, and caused them much pain.*

Indians who continued to worship their old gods could be burned at the stake or hanged.

Friars burning images of Mexican gods, brought to them by the Indians on the right. The old gods are shown going up in smoke.

see that the Spaniards always won in battle and that their enemies died of diseases like smallpox. They reasoned that the white men's gods were more powerful than their own, and came forward by the thousands to be baptized.

Despite Christianity, many old beliefs did survive. The old and the new religions became mixed together. For example, instead of offering flowers and incense to the old gods, people offered them to the Virgin Mary and the saints. In the villages, many of the old gods were worshiped alongside Jesus Christ. Today, Maya farmers in Yucatan still pray to their rain gods when their fields need water.

# Life in Spanish America

The friars thought that Indians should dress like Europeans, in trousers instead of loincloths and capes.

*Opposite* An Inca drawing showing how the people of Peru irrigated, or watered, their fields. The Inca irrigation canals were neglected under Spanish rule.

Once the fighting was over, the conquistadors settled down to rule their new lands. The most important Spaniards were given large numbers of Indians to work for them. As well as working on the Spaniards' farms and in their mines, the Indians were kept busy building new cities – Mexico City was built on the site of Tenochtitlan. They also had to pay tribute to the Spaniards in goods such as woven cloth.

The American mines were a great source of wealth for Spain. A fifth of all the gold and silver mined was set aside for the Spanish king. Twice a year, his fleet would sail across the sea from America, loaded with treasure.

The king and the Church did their best to protect the Indians from cruel treatment. Even so, Spanish rule had a terrible effect on Indian life. The conquistadors were more interested in getting rich quickly than in taking care of the Indians. Thousands were worked to death in the mines. Meanwhile, their fields were neglected. The Incas' irrigation canals were left to crumble. Without water, the fields of Peru stopped producing food.

Worst of all were the European diseases. Millions of people died of smallpox, measles, and influenza. When Cortés arrived in Mexico in 1519, more than 20 million Indians lived there; by 1620, there were not even one million left.

Pedro de Cieza de Leon was one Spaniard who hated what his people had done in Peru. He wrote:

*It is no small sorrow to reflect that we Christians have destroyed so many kingdoms. For wherever Christians have passed, conquering and discovering, it seems as though a fire has gone, eating up everything.*

# GLOSSARY

**Atahuallpa** (say atta-wall-pa) The Inca ruler of Peru in 1532.

**Aztecs** The people who ruled over the Aztec Empire (part of what is now Mexico) between 1420 and 1521. They called themselves the "Mexica," from which comes the modern name "Mexico." They are called Aztecs after the place they originally came from, Aztlan.

**Conquistador** (say con-kiss-tah-dor) A Spanish word meaning "conqueror." The name given to the Spaniards who conquered large parts of the Americas in the 1500s.

**Cuauhtemoc** (say kwow-tay-mok) This means "Falling Eagle," and was the name of the last Aztec ruler.

**Friar** A Christian holy man. Spanish friars traveled to America to persuade the people there to become Christians. In order to convert the people, many friars learned their languages. They also wrote down much of the history and beliefs of the people of America.

**Hispaniola** The name that Christopher Columbus gave to the first Caribbean island settled by the Spanish. Today the island is two countries – Haiti and the Dominican Republic.

**Huitzilopochtli** (say weet-zill-o-potch-tlee) This means "Blue Hummingbird of the South." It was the name of the Aztec god of war and the rising sun. He was usually shown as a warrior, painted blue, holding a magic weapon, a snake of fire.

**Inca** The word *Inca* means "Lord" and was the title of the rulers of Peru. This name was later given to the people of Peru themselves. In fact, they called themselves the *Quechua* (say kay-choo-ah).

**Maya** (say my-a) The people of Guatemala and Yucatan. Maya civilization was much older than Aztec or Inca. A thousand years before the Spanish arrived, the Maya were building cities. Today, there are still around four million Maya in Central America.

**Missionaries** People who travel to different places to spread their own religion.

**Montezuma** (say mon-tuh-zoo-mah) This means "He frowns like a lord" or "Angry Lord," and was the name of the Aztec ruler in 1519.

*Quipus* (say kee-poos) An Inca method of keeping records using different-colored string, tied into knots. The color of the string and the number and position of the knots all meant something. The word *quipu* means "knot."

**Tainos** The native people who lived on Hispaniola, Cuba, and other islands in the Caribbean.

**Tenochtitlan** (say te-notch-tit-lan) This means "Cactus Rock." It was the capital city of the Aztecs, built in the middle of Lake Texcoco. It was rebuilt by the Spaniards as Mexico City.

**Tlaloc** (say tlah-lock) Tlaloc was the rain god, worshiped by the Aztecs and all the other people of Mexico. He is easy to recognize – in most carvings and paintings he is shown with goggle eyes and long teeth.

**Tlaxcala** (say tlash-ca-la) This means "Place of Bread," and was a town in Mexico. The Tlaxcalans were enemies of the Aztecs and helped the Spaniards to fight them.

**Tribute** Money or other valuables paid to a powerful ruler by those who are less powerful.

# BOOKS TO READ

Chrisp, Peter. *Voyages to the New World.* Explorations & Encounters. New York: Thomson Learning, 1993.

Greene, Jacqueline D. *The Maya.* First Books. New York: Franklin Watts, 1992.

Hicks, Peter. *The Aztecs.* Look Into the Past. New York: Thomson Learning, 1993.

Kendall, Sarita. *The Incas.* New York: Macmillan Children's Book Group, 1992.

Marrin, Albert. *Aztecs and Spaniards: Cortés and the Conquest of Mexico.* New York: Atheneum Children's Books, 1986.

Newman, Shirlee P. *The Incas.* First Books. New York: Franklin Watts, 1992.

Wood, Tim. *The Aztecs.* New York: Viking Children's Books, 1992.

# INDEX